BATHROOMS

BATHROOMS

A PRACTICAL GUIDE TO DESIGN
AND DECOR FOR YOUR HOME

FAY SWEET

MEREHURST

First published in 1995 by Merehurst Limited,
Ferry House, 51-57 Lacy Road, Putney, London SW15 1PR

Copyright © Merehurst Limited 1995

ISBN 1 85391 492 4

A catalogue record of this book is available from
the British Library

Designed by Ivor Claydon
Special photography on pages
4, 47 and 55 by Lu Jeffery
Styling by Kate Hardy
Illustrated by Corinne and Ray Burrows

Typesetting by Cameron Typesetting
Colour separation by P & W Graphics, Singapore
Printed in Italy by Canale SpA

ACKNOWLEDGMENTS

Robert Harding Syndication supplied transparencies on pages 2 & 41
by Polly Wreford, Country Homes & Interiors; page 9 by Tim Beddow,
Homes & Gardens; page 11 by T. Imrie, Ideal Home; pages 13 & 39
by James Merrell, Homes & Gardens; pages 15, 18, 24, 37,
42 & 43 by Trevor Richards, Homes & Gardens; page 27 by S. Powell,
Ideal Home; page 31 by James Merrell, Definitions; page 63 by
Les Mehan, Ideal Home.

Elizabeth Whiting & Associates supplied transparencies on page 4 by
Nadia McKenzie; page 7 by Michael Crockett; page 21 by Rodney Hyett;
page 35 by Michael Dunne; page 53 by Spike Powell.

Photography on page 1 by G. Chabaneix, Marie Claire Ideas; pages 3, 5,
57 & 59 supplied by Crown Paints; pages 5 & 28 supplied by C.P. Hart
Group; pages 4 & 6 supplied by Fired Earth; pages 17, 33 & 45 by
Paul Ryan, International Interiors; pages 23, 25, 26 & 29 supplied by
Ideal Standard; pages 49 and 61 supplied by The Stencil Store; page 51
supplied by Dulux.

Fay Sweet would like to thank Ideal Standard, British Bathroom Council,
The Stencil Store, Antico, Armitage Shanks, Twyfords, Radiating Style,
C.P. Hart, Dulux, Crown Paints, & Eco Paints.

Contents

Introduction

Ever since man first dipped his toes in the sea, he has enjoyed bathing. The Greeks and Romans elevated the experience to an art form and have bequeathed a rich architectural legacy of spa baths and towns.

Our love of bathing remains as strong as ever and, with the help of vast improvements in modern plumbing and the availability of a huge choice of furnishings and fittings, the bathroom has become not just a place for personal hygiene but also for relaxation and indulgence in unashamed luxury.

Above all, the bathroom should be comfortable, welcoming and practical. Here we can spring to life with an invigorating shower or lie back in warm, foaming, scented waters to soothe mind and body after the rigours of a hard day. Here, too, we can unleash our decorating fantasies and create rooms with intriguing themes based on such varied subjects as the seaside, Roman spas, Arabic opulence, a desert oasis, Edwardian stylishness, a fantasy grotto or, perhaps, a luxurious stream-lined Art Deco hotel.

However, as well as being decorative, the bathroom must be able to withstand a great deal of wear and tear. Many of us will have to share the room with the rest of the family; we may need to fit in a washing machine, airing cupboard and linen store. If there is space, you may even decide to incorporate a mini gym. No matter what style you choose, the bathroom must be functional, hard-wearing and easy to clean.

In this book we will offer practical design and decorating guidelines and suggestions to help you make the most of your space and budget and create a bathroom that will be a pleasure to use for many years to come.

Less is more. Restrained use of decoration can be extremely elegant. The simplicity of this plain white bathroom suite and wall tiling is offset by the three pretty plates, the ceramic tile border and fine wallpaper border around the top of the room.

Your Bathroom

The essence of all good design is thoughtful planning and research. So before you make any alterations to your bathroom it is important to consider what already exists and how it might saved or changed. Once a bathroom suite is fixed in place, it is a costly business moving it around. Careful thought at the start of the job can save a great deal of money later.

Invest in a notebook, a folder for the many brochures you are sure to gather and some graph paper to draw a diagram of your bathroom to scale: then cut out pieces to the shape and size of sanitary ware and move them around on the paper until they describe your ideal layout.

At the start take a long hard look at the room; take note of its shape, height, size and fixtures and fittings.

What space do I have to work with?

The first question should be whether the bathroom is in the right place. Is it in a very large room that would be better used as a bedroom? Alternatively, if your bathroom is very small, do you have a spare room that could be converted into a larger bathroom? Can you remove a wall between the bathroom and adjoining lavatory to make more space? How about moving a partition wall and taking space from a neighbouring bedroom?

If members of your household all want to use the bathroom at the same time, consider the possibility of easing the morning or evening rush by installing a free-standing shower or wash-hand basin in a bedroom. Do you have the luxury of space for a small en suite bathroom? If you have a separate cloakroom, is there room there for a shower? Does it make sense to remove the lavatory from the bathroom and locate it elsewhere to make more room?

The size and arrangement of your existing bathroom, plus the siting of windows and doors, will play a key role in how it is used. Take accurate measurements so that you know exactly what you are dealing with. Measure floor to ceiling height as well as length and breadth. Draw a rough plan and mark in doors and windows, and the current plumbing arrangements, too. It is always a good idea to have all these measurements to hand when you go shopping.

Let us start with the very smallest of bathrooms. Unless you delight in chaos, or deliberately choose a style of decor that is vivacious and incorporates hoards of curious objects, a tiny space is best kept plain and simple.

There is certainly something very satisfying about making the most of a tiny space - and plenty of inspiration can be found by looking at bathrooms on board boats and barges and even in caravans. Clean, smooth lines, compact items of sanitary ware, fitted cupboards and light colours all open out a space. Make the most of any natural light. It may be possible to enlarge the window or, if your bathroom is at the top of the house, fit a skylight.

Ultimate luxury, the pretty open shelves are practical as well as decorative as they offer valuable storage space together with the opportunity to show off beautiful bottles and dishes. The cupboard unit, given a marble-effect paint finish, contains the lavatory cistern. An upholstered chair and huge vase of flowers add a lavish touch.

A large bathroom is, of course, the most flexible of all. Here you will have room to experiment and really wallow in luxury. Fit in that shower or second wash-hand basin you have always wanted. Perhaps you can make a feature of a beautiful bath and place it right in the centre of the room.

How will the bathroom be used?

Are you the sort of person who enjoys long, luxurious baths, or do you prefer quick, refreshing showers? Do you have a large bathroom that could accommodate a home sauna, a collection of gym equipment or a humble exercise bicycle?

If you have a small budget for renovating your house or apartment, there is little to be gained by spending most of it on an expensive bathroom. If you can happily live with the existing suite, your time, effort and money will be best spent smartening up the room with some new tiles, a coat of fresh paint and good lighting. An extremely smart, top-quality bathroom can enhance the value of your property but, if you plan to stay in your current home for just a short time then a large investment is almost certainly unwise.

Young children, the elderly and disabled can bring all sorts of different needs. Children will want to be independent and use the lavatory and basin by themselves. This is made easy by providing them with a small step on which they can stand. Someone suffering from arthritis may find ordinary taps difficult to use, so look out for types that are designed for ease of use. A wide doorway is necessary for a wheelchair user. Pay special attention at this point to finishes, too. The bathroom is furnished with hard objects that will cause injury in the case of a fall. Consider non-slip flooring and incorporate rounded edges where possible.

What would I most like to change?

This is the time to crystallise your thoughts. To be thorough, think more broadly than the good and bad elements of your own bathroom, and remember what you liked and disliked about your last bathroom and your friends' and family's bathrooms.

A good place to start is the sanitary ware. Do you like the suite in your existing bathroom; if not, what sort of thing do you like? Would you like a double-bowl wash-hand basin? What style of bathroom do you prefer: do you like very functional,

sleek, ceramic-tiled rooms, or perhaps something a little softer with wood panelling on the walls, gentle lighting, carpet or cushioned vinyl on the floor and an upholstered easy chair? If your current bathroom has fitted units already, do you like the doors and handles? If not, perhaps these can be painted or replaced. Changing doors can transform a room easily and inexpensively. If you are aiming for a nautical look, then try plain pine with brass catches; if you want something a little more stream-lined, there are plenty of smooth-finished, melamine-faced doors available in a multitude of colours.

The colour scheme may be dictated by the sanitary ware. If you have chosen to keep the existing suite then you may like to devise a complementary scheme. The more adventurous could try a daring contrast: sunshine yellow to go with a

The addition of wood textures makes a handsome bathroom. The bath panel is given a painted wood grain effect which serves to complement the wooden chair and flooring. Added interest is given to the plain creamy walls with the chequered tile pattern.

green suite or purple to offset pink. If you are unsure, neutral colours such as white and cream are a safe bet and extremely easy to live with until you feel inspired by beautiful tiles or wallpaper. Alternatively, if you have a dark bathroom you might like to transform it into a light, white space; or you could play on the darkness and turn it into an intriguing, dark cavern. Do you like hot colours such as reds and oranges, or cool tones of blue and green; or bright colours like turquoise and fluorescent pink? Do you have a favourite item - an exotic pot plant, a decorative cupboard, a chair, painting or curtains - that you would like to build a colour scheme around?

Once you have an idea of colours and styles, begin to think about finishes. There is a huge choice of bathroom wall coverings and floorings and many of the options will be discussed later in this book (see pages 36-9). In the meantime, visit plenty of showrooms, compare prices and ask friends how they came to choose their particular flooring or wallpaper and whether they are happy with it. Ask if their finishes were easy to install, whether they are hard wearing and if there are any drawbacks. For example, ceramic floor tiles may look great, but they can be cold to walk on barefoot.

Lighting can be extremely difficult to get just right (see pages 34-5). For the time being, ask yourself whether you like side lighting or a central lamp. Would ceiling-recessed fittings be a good idea? Do you like to wash in bright, crisp light, or a slightly softer glow?

Finally, consider whether you can afford to invest in a water softener. They can be expensive to install, but will provide you with wonderfully soft water and will save many problems with lime scale furring up pipes and staining sanitary ware. Also decide what sort of heating might be appropriate and whether you need additional ventilation to cope with condensation.

What can I achieve within my budget?

Now comes the moment of reckoning. Take your list of 'likes' and mark it up in order of priority. Once you have worked out your order of works, estimate how much you need to spend on each alteration and change.

With so many temptations in the showroom, it is all too easy to overspend so be absolutely clear about what you can afford. Build in an emergency fund of perhaps ten per cent for unexpected eventualities.

If your bathroom looks fine as it is, but you would like additional facilities, consider putting a shower unit in the bedroom or an extra lavatory under the stairs. If you are planning to live with this bathroom for just a short time, do not be tempted to spend a fortune. Even if you are expecting to stay for five years, it is still worth considering inexpensive but effective options.

Finally, make yourself the promise that you will shop around and compare prices. Always aim to collect three quotes for any work to be carried out and never take the first quote you are offered. It is important to be well prepared, and, above all, to be realistic about what you can achieve.

Drama in black and white is enhanced by the powerful pattern of Roman heads on the wallpaper and the bold floor tiles. Stainless steel details work extremely well with the monochrome decor. Crisp, white towels are a must after taking an invigorating shower.

Bathroom Planning and Design

There are few hard and fast rules in bathroom planning and design. The simple guidelines are that the room should be functional, waterproof, attractive and comfortable.

The first consideration is the layout of your suite. If you have decided to keep your existing sanitary ware, but would like to change the arrangement, bear in mind the position of the waste pipe. It is always a good idea to try and locate bath, lavatory and wash-hand basin, and therefore the pipes, along the outside wall. Of course, a straight line of bowls may not look particularly attractive, nor will it necessarily be possible to run everything along one wall; however, in general, the further you move the bath or lavatory from the waste pipe, the greater the installation cost. Should it be absolutely necessary to locate the lavatory a long distance away, it may be worth asking professional advice about whether it is necessary to install a macerator – this is an electrically-powered unit that will pump waste to its destination.

Your budget and size of room will, of course, dictate just how much reorganisation you can carry out. Careful thought at this stage will save problems and expense later. Remember to refer to your notes on how you want to use the space. Always seek professional advice if you are unsure.

As you are drawing-up plans, keep in mind how you and others will use the room. For example, by keeping all the sanitary ware in a contained area at one end or side of the room, you will free up plenty of space for storage or for a laundry area. Always make sure you leave a sensible working space around sanitary ware. For example, you will need room by the side of the bath for drying yourself or for kneeling to wash children. Elderly or disabled bathers may need more generous space to enable them to get in and out of the bath safely. The same guidelines apply to the wash-hand basin, lavatory, bidet and shower. Wall-fixed grab rails can also ensure safe movement around the room.

It is also important to consider the needs of those who are very tall or very short. Sanitary ware and fitted units are designed for adults of average height. If you are very tall, one solution to the height problem is to raise the wash-hand basin. If you are short, you could remove fitted unit bases to lower the overall height. Also remember that mirrors will have to be placed so that everyone can use them. The disadvantage of tailoring your bathroom so specifically is that prospective house buyers may take exception to your alterations.

To help you in your planning and design, we will now discuss some ideas for three typical bathroom shapes.

The Long, Narrow Bathroom

This shape of room almost inevitably means that you will be obliged to place your sanitary ware in a line. The configuration will work in almost any way: lavatory, bath

The simplicity of this modern bathroom is achieved by dispensing with all clutter. The floor is of plain, stripped boards, the bath is encased in a hoop of stainless steel, and storage space is hidden by an entire wall of mirrored unit doors which help to reflect light and give a greater sense of space. The lavatory is tucked in behind a mosaic-tiled false wall.

then wash-hand basin, or wash-hand basin and lavatory side by side followed by the bath. This second line up occupies slightly less space than the former because basin and lavatory can be squeezed up close. The assumption is that you will require less working space around them because they are unlikely to be used simultaneously.

If the room is very long, you may have space for a shower and/or bidet too. As opportunities for storage are likely to be limited, consider fitting your wash-hand basin into a cupboard or vanity unit. If you choose to make a feature of the room's elongated shape, fit a continuous line of units down one side to hold your sanitary ware, and tile walls and floor. Always make sure that there is easy maintenance access to pipes hidden by units. Decorative lines of tiles, or wallpaper borders running lengthways through the space, will give the effect of stretching the room yet further.

If you prefer to break up the line effect, fit a narrow shelving unit on the wall opposite the bath and basin. This could be in the form of a book case and is ideal for storing toiletries and plants. Also consider a wall-fixed, heated towel rail, a decorative tile mural, a large

mirror or perhaps a painting.

Another excellent idea to break up the row effect is to build in a waist-height screen at either or both ends of the bath. This can be tiled and will not only give you extra shelf space, but also screen the lavatory. If there is space, it can be extended to ceiling height and form one side of a shower cubicle.

Where the room is wide enough, you may choose to fix the wash-hand basin or lavatory at the far end. If the room is wider still, you will probably be able to place the bath widthways across the room. This is always a very neat solution. Baths are now available in many different lengths, so ask around for the size you require.

The Tiny Bathroom

The smallest bathrooms can also be the most efficient. There certainly will not be space to waste and, if the budget allows, you may be able to splash out on more exotic finishes - marble, for example - that you would not be able to afford to furnish a larger space. En suite bathrooms are usually fairly compact, so this section will apply to those too.

Small-sized wash-hand basins will gain you a little extra room,

as will slim, fitted units and slim-line lavatory cisterns. Wall-hung basins and lavatories will provide you with extra floor space.

For more substantial space gains, it may be possible to fit a smaller bath. Re-hanging an inward opening door to make it outward opening will reclaim extra floor space. Could you remove the bath altogether and replace it with a shower? This latter suggestion deserves very careful consideration. It could slightly deter a prospective buyer if he or she is particularly partial to taking baths.

If there is no opportunity to poach more space then clearly you must make the most of what you have. Fitted units, both floor and wall fixed, will give the room a stream-lined, more spacious feel and provide valuable storage capacity. Boxing in plumbing will tidy up pipework and may provide you with a useful bench seat or small cupboard, but remember to ensure access for maintenance.

Colour is an important factor too (see pages 30-3). Light-coloured rooms will appear larger than dark ones. By the same token, additional natural light in the form of a larger window or a skylight can enhance the feeling of space.

The Square Bathroom

This shape really is the ideal and provides the opportunity for many different layouts. Most bathroom designs start with the bath; if it is placed lengthways against one wall and there is extra space, you may like to consider fitting a separate shower, bidet or a storage cupboard to complete the run. Next, decide on positions for the lavatory and wash-hand basin. As mentioned earlier, the lavatory is best placed close to the waste pipe to ensure efficient drainage. The basin can be fitted alongside or opposite. The door position will probably dictate the site. Ensure the door can open without crashing into the sanitary ware - chips and cracks can be irreparable.

If you have the luxury of a generous-sized space, the bath can be turned to point into the centre of the room with the taps end only against the wall.

Space Planning

Disciplined and thoughtful space planning really makes the most of any bathroom. As a general rule, a standard bath will need around 80cm (32 in) floor space along the long side for drying yourself or for kneeling and bathing infants; a lavatory or bidet requires around 80cm (32 in) floor space in front and 70cm (28 in) widthways for comfortable use; a wash-hand basin needs some 80cm (32 in) in front for bending space and a shower will need the same in front for drying. These space allowances can overlap as it is usual for only one person at a time to use the room. If you have very young children, think about

The simple decorative effect of square window panes is echoed in white tiling around the bath and on the floor. The coolness of this all-white room is given a touch of warmth with the low-level wooden table and its collection of intriguing objects.

incorporating space for changing nappies. Also build in extra space to manoeuvre for those who may be wheelchair bound.

Always think carefully about the positions of protruding fixtures such as lavatory-roll holders and towel rails. It can be both annoying and dangerous constantly to bump into these. Once you have worked out the first draft of your plan, it is a good idea to call in the professionals for advice and quotes. It is best to enlist the help of a registered plumber and to collect together three quotes. The cheapest will not necessarily be the best. Select a plumber who you like, who understands your needs, and who has quoted a fair price for the job.

Ventilation

A build-up of condensation is undesirable, not just aesthetically (it can produce unsightly black mould marks)

Raise the temperature with a palatte of pulsating, rich earthy colours. Unusual decoration based on Inca designs is used liberally in wall murals, borders and on the bath panel. The complex geometric patterns are echoed on the textured fabrics of the rugs and the throw over the sofa.

but also structurally, as it can rot and cause material damage to walls, window frames and floors. The solution is to ensure your bathroom is adequately ventilated. This can be achieved by fitting simple window vents. However, if the problem is acute, you may need to install an electrically-powered extractor fan; the sort recommended for bathrooms are usually activated by the light-pull cord and switch off automatically. A powerful ventilator is essential, and required by law, in a bathroom without windows.

Storage

Take stock of all those items that you would like to store in your bathroom. If you are lucky enough to have an airing cupboard, you will probably have ready-made linen storage. You may want to build in space for toiletries, cosmetics, medicines, cleaning materials, spare lavatory paper, and perhaps dirty linen.

In recent years, many manufacturers have borrowed from the excellent ideas of fitted kitchen specialists and have devised many ranges of fitted bathroom units. These are available in a wide variety of finishes and styles and offer all sorts of storage details such as swing-out drawers, pull-out

shelving, in-built shelves, inset lighting and dirty linen baskets.

At the very least, you will probably need a lockable medicine cupboard, or one that is well out of the reach of children. Some storage for toiletries and cosmetics is a good idea. How about a place for storing bathroom cleaning materials; this can be found under the basin or perhaps in a concealed panel under the bath?

However, if you prefer an unfitted bathroom, let your imagination run riot. You may like to opt for a more random selection of cupboards and shelves. An old sideboard will provide excellent towel storage space - paint it to match your scheme; a pine kitchen dresser or wardrobe will carry just about anything you could possibly need in a bathroom; bookcases can help you tidy everything away.

Because so many bathroom accessories and toiletries are attractive, open shelving looks great. Choose glass, wood, or even rust-proof metal.

Finishes for Cupboards and Counter Tops

The finishes you choose will help to set the style of your bathroom. As a guide, if you want to create a warm, comfortable feel then choose from a palette of natural materials, particularly woods. For an efficient, hygienic style of bathroom, select smooth-finish laminates.

To transform old bathroom units, it is now possible to buy and fit new doors. As long as your cupboards are sound and of a standard size, this can save a great deal of unnecessary expense and wasted materials in buying entirely new units. You can even achieve a simple face lift by replacing old handles.

Counter tops are available in dozens of materials, textures and patterns. One of the most popular, practical and least expensive is laminate. This man-made material copes well with the wear and tear of bathroom life as it is tough, waterproof, hygienic, scratch and stain resistant. More expensive man-made materials include Corian, a type of artificial stone. Like laminate, it is hard-wearing, easily wiped clean, water and heat resistant. Unlike laminate, it is a solid material that can be cut and shaped to provide a smooth and seamless surface.

Woods such as beech and maple have an enduring appeal and are easily cut to the required size and shape. When oiled or varnished they are water resistant but require occasional maintenance to keep them looking good. If you look after it properly, wood will improve with age. Always check the source of the wood you are buying - imported hardwoods may have been cut from rain forests or other unsustainable sources.

Planning Tips

• Always use registered plumbers and electricians.

• A small box enables young children to reach and use the wash-hand basin safely. Ensure, however, that they cannot use this to reach medicines which should be kept in a locked cupboard. Cleaning materials must be kept well out of reach.

• Only use electrical appliances and switches recommended for use in the bathroom.

• Keep all electrical appliances well away from water.

• Consider fitting hand grips or rails to make it easier for the young, elderly and disabled to get in and out of bath.

• A small plastic stool or flap-down seat can make it easier for the young and the elderly to enjoy a shower.

• When looking for showers, check the one you have chosen has in-built temperature stabilisation or thermostatic control - this will prevent shower users from being scalded or chilled.

• Dripping taps waste water and can cause lime-scale stains - replace the washers as soon as the problem starts.

• It is now possible to buy mirrors that contain a heat element to prevent them from misting.

• Always check your local bye laws before making major alterations to rooms and plumbing. Your plans may require special approval.

• To cut down on heating bills, insulate your hot water tank with a jacket that is at least 8cm (3 ¼ in) thick. Line behind radiators with silver foil to reflect heat back into the room and turn down your central heating and hot water thermostat just one degree.

An in-built shelf unit offers neat and useful storage space in this modern-style bathroom. The bathtub is housed in a mosaic tiled recess where shower splashes are contained by the ingenious pivoting shower screen.

Sanitary Ware

If you have the good fortune to be looking for new sanitary ware, be prepared to be spoilt for choice. During recent years manufacturers have produced collections in every style imaginable. Whether your taste is for a decorative Victorian bathroom, smart Edwardian suites, angular Art Deco, frivolous shell shapes, sleek high tech, or for the most recent, smooth, rounded, ergonomically formed shapes, with a little hunting around you are sure to be able to find a suite to suit you.

Think carefully before you buy; bathroom suites can be very expensive. It is also worth checking the weight of items, especially cast-iron baths, to make sure that your floors can take the strain. Also, if you opt for a wall-hung lavatory and bidet, ensure your walls are sound.

When making your decisions, it is always a good idea to try out the items for size and comfort. You may feel a little foolish lying flat out in an empty bath in the showroom, but it is well worth the temporary embarrassment to find one that is really comfortable. Sit on the lavatory and imagine washing in the basin. Every piece of sanitary ware has its own distinctive shape and peculiarities; make sure they work with your own body. It would be a terrible mistake to spend a small fortune buying and fitting a bathroom suite, only to discover that you knocked your elbow on the sculpted armrest of the bath every time you got in and out.

The Bath

The bath has undergone a massive personality change since the era of the tin tub. In the early days, it was a purely functional receptacle that was hauled in front of the fire once a week for a quick wash down. It was hardly the place to enjoy a long, lingering soak.

Your main considerations when buying a bath are the size you need, the shape and style, the comfort factor, the position and type of tap holes and the material in which it is made. The size should be evident from your plan; however, you will be offered a choice of different internal shapes. Try them out; they will vary in depth, width, length and contours. If you enjoy a soak in really deep water, check the height of the waste outlet. Special shapes - baths with low sides, for example - are designed for the elderly or disabled. A good range of easy-to-operate taps is also now on offer, as are all shapes and sizes of grab rails to make it easy getting in and out of the bath.

The style you buy is entirely up to you. Do you want a period look, a free-standing bath with exposed feet, a sunken bath (only realistic for ground-floor bathrooms), or something that can be boxed in? If you are looking for a genuine cast-iron Victorian or Edwardian period article, try one of the many architectural salvage yards that have sprung up in most large towns and cities. Before parting with your cash, check it inside and out very carefully for scratches, chips and cracks. It is possible to repair small dents and to have the bath resurfaced, but serious flaws, cracks especially, are terminal.

Elegant and simple sanitaryware which fits neatly into a smooth faced unit. This sort of arrangement is not only a great space saver, but also disguises ugly pipework and cistern and provides additional, valuable storage space.

If you would like a bath with an over-head shower, consider the shapes that have a flat, slightly squared-off bed at the shower end - this makes it a great deal easier and safer to use the shower. Check on types that incorporate non-slip surfaces. Or, perhaps your heart is set on a corner-fitting bath? These take up slightly more room than the regular, rectangular shape; make sure you have allowed for the difference in your plans.

If your budget allows, you have the option to buy baths with integrated whirlpools and spa features, sold with the claim that they will gently massage and tone our aching muscles and joints. While the medical profession may reserve judgement on the actual physical benefits, few can deny that a bath full of swirling, frothing water is fun and can make you feel great. This type of bath is available in a choice of three different actions: the whirlpool, which simply recirculates the bath water, spa baths which pump air through water, and the whirlpool spa which pumps a mixture of air and water. Take great care in making

The classic Victorian-style roll-top bath tub and pedestal basin remain perennial favourites. They are generous in size and always look smart. The handsome bath is given pride of place and becomes the main focus of the room. Pretty mosaic tiles provide decorative panels on the otherwise plain walls.

your choice to ensure the model meets safety regulations and enlist the help of an expert for correct installation.

The style of taps will depend on your taste, but remember that it is vital to ensure that the bath and taps are compatible. Some baths are sold with three holes for taps and a central spout, some are sold with just one hole for a monobloc (a single spout with handles attached at the sides), and some have no holes at all and are intended for those bathrooms that have taps and spout fixed to the wall. You might consider the baths sold with a central or corner-mounted tap fixing and plug hole – then no one has to sit at the taps end!

Baths are available in several materials; they are as follows:

Acrylic This material is extremely popular; it will not rust or corrode and is very light. Acrylic baths are vacuum formed from a thin sheet of material that is usually reinforced underneath with glass fibre. The thicknesses can range from around 3mm (¼ in) up to 10mm (½ in). These baths have the additional advantages of being warm to the touch; they keep water warmer for longer and are easily wiped clean.

Steel This is tough and hardwearing and is coated with porcelain or vitreous enamel. The steel used for baths is usually between 1.5mm (⅛ in) and 3mm (¼ in) thick. For the most rigid structure, buy the thickest that you can afford.

Cast iron A very heavy and hardwearing material, cast iron is usually coated in a softer enamel than those used on steel. Abrasive cleaners should not be used on this type of bath. The disadvantage of cast iron is that water cools rapidly.

The Lavatory

Just about all lavatories are now made in vitreous china. This is a tough, hardwearing, stain-resistant material, but it can chip and may even crack if given a hefty knock.

The main consideration when choosing a lavatory is whether you would like a floor- or wall-mounted model. As mentioned earlier, the wall-mounted version frees floor space and, because it is fairly heavy and can weigh around 20kg (40 lb), should only be fitted to a sound wall.

The variety of styles matches that on offer for baths. Take note of the position of the cistern as this can be crucial to your efficient use of room; there are space- and water-saving options. Victorian and Edwardian-style models have a high-level cistern and the flush is operated by a pull chain. The more modern cisterns fit directly behind the bowl and are operated by a handle. These cisterns are available in a variety of designs: there are those where the cistern is left on show and others where it is designed to be concealed in a unit that also contains pipe work. It is also possible to buy very slim cisterns that can fit into the depth of a wall; these are extremely water efficient.

The Wash-hand Basin

Like the lavatory, these are almost always made in vitreous china. Basins are available in all sorts of shapes and sizes, from corner-fitted models, square, oval and round pedestal or wall-hung types, to those which fit or are semi-inset into vanity units. You can get some wash-hand basins that are formed in a continuous piece with wide counter areas at either side and others which come as free-standing wash stands. If you can afford the space, it is usually best to get a really large basin, and a shallow bowl will help you save on water consumption.

The Shower

This is the most cost-, energy- and water-effective way of staying clean. A shower can use just one quarter of the water required to fill a bath.

The lovely rounded forms of the taps and waterspout complement the shape of this wash-hand basin.

When you are looking at showers, check that the controls are easy to read and to understand. Consider what sort of doors or screens are best for your bathroom. If water pressure is low, it is best to fit a shower with pump; check this with your plumber. Also ask if you need a larger water-storage tank.

It is advisable to hire a professional fitter. It is most important to ensure the unit is completely waterproof. Shower water is extremely invasive; it can wear away grout and will find many means of escape. Unless the water is contained, it will cause damaging mould and rot.

If you are buying a shower for the first time, the choice can be bewildering. There are three main choices for position: over the bath, in a tiled cubicle, or in a free-standing unit.

Next comes the type of system. These are grouped under three main headings:

Electric or Gas This is the most economical option. Firstly, the units are quick and easy to install as they are simply connected to the cold-water mains. Secondly, hot water is instantaneous as it is heated as it passes through the shower unit; this means you do not need to heat up an entire tank of water and that you can have hot showers when the rest of your hot water system is switched off.

The disadvantage of this type of shower is that it is slower to work when the weather is cold because it takes longer to heat up the cold incoming water. As a general rule, the higher the kilowatt rating (this is usually between 7.5 kW and 9 kW), the higher the flow rate.

Most shower systems are now available with multi-function shower heads that allow you to regulate the flow of water. If you live in a hard-water area, it is also worth checking to see if the head is lime-scale resistant or, at the very least, easily cleaned.

Mixer This has a higher flow rate than the electric or gas shower, as the mixer draws from both the hot and cold household supplies and then mixes them for you. It can also be more costly to install than the electric shower and relies on hot water being available at the time when you want to shower. With the addition of a pump to boost the flow rate, you can turn your mixer into a power shower (see below); the pump also dispenses with the need to ensure adequate gravity pressure to keep water flowing.

The softly rounded contours of this basin are stylish in any bathroom setting. Because the basin has no awkward sharp corners it is a particularly good choice in a family bathroom.

Make sure the mixer control knob is easy to use and read. Some have separate controls to regulate flow and temperature. The temperature control can be very useful to prevent scalding, as it should keep the water temperature constant within one degree centigrade no matter what other taps are switched on in the house. A normal flow will be between 8 and 13 litres (between 2 and 3 gallons approximately) per minute. The most powerful will pump up to 18 litres (4 gallons) per minute.

Power This is a pump-assisted mixer shower. It draws both hot and cold from the household supply and uses more water than either the electric or mixer types. If you are considering installing one of these, make sure the drain hole in your shower tray can cope with volume of water and is kept free of obstructions.

The power shower, although more expensive to install and run, is the ultimate in exhilarating showering and you can finely control the flow of water from gentle, frothy champagne

This cluttered cloakroom has a welcoming, informal rural appeal. Hats, wicker baskets and a wooden cupboard add to the interesting collection of textures and colours found in the tiled floor, painted half-panelled walls and soft curtain fabric.

bubbles to tingling needle jets. The experience can be enhanced by the addition of body sprays positioned in the wall.

The Shower Enclosure

Shower curtains are very reasonably priced, they are available in many attractive designs and they can work well

if used properly. However, unless they are thoroughly cleaned and dried on a regular basis, they will become slimy and mouldy. Some types of curtain can be washed in the washing machine.

Currently, the most popular choice for the shower enclosure is a screen or door. Screens are manufactured in glass or

Almost romantically lit matching floor-standing bidet and WC. Perhaps the ultimate in sanitary elegance, these were manufactured in Germany and form part of the suite in a bathroom by the French interior designer, Philippe Starck.

acrylic; avoid materials with ridges as these will harbour dirt. Ensure they form a water-tight fit with the top of your bath (especially roll tops) or shower tray. They are easy to clean and durable. If you choose a folding screen, make sure that it folds inwards over the bath to prevent water dripping on the floor.

The same attention to water tightness applies to shower cubicles. Ensure all joints are sealed and that doors fit closely.

The Shower Tray

For the free-standing shower, a good, solid tray is essential. Most trays are manufactured in either ceramic or acrylic and the most popular are square shaped. Some are made with a small up-stand which fits against the wall and ensures a water-tight seal with the surrounding tiles. Trays need to be completely rigid and must be laid on a solid base to prevent any movement. If you choose an acrylic model, check that it does not move - this is easily achieved by standing in the tray and rocking from foot to foot. It should also have adjustable feet so that it can be laid level.

If you opt to buy a tailor-made shower enclosure, ensure it is compatible with the tray.

The Bidet

Bidets are becoming increasingly popular and, like lavatories and wash-hand

basins, are usually made in vitreous china. They can be wall or floor fixed. If you choose a wall-mounted model, check your wall is strong enough to support the weight.

The water arrives in a choice of three ways: an under-rim supply which flows down the side of the bowl, an ascending spray, or an over-rim supply. The latter resembles a regular mixer tap and is the most popular.

The Taps

Just like bathroom suites, these come in every conceivable style: the old-fashioned cross-head shape, laboratory-style lever operated, acrylic-capped pillar taps, bath/shower mixers, three-piece mixers and monobloc. You can buy single-stem units, wall-fixed taps and the

Victorian-style 'telephone' unit, incorporating taps, bath/shower lever and shower head. Some taps are specially designed to make them easy to use and particularly suitable for the elderly or disabled. Taps are available in many finishes: chrome, nickel, brass, gold. Be sure to choose one that matches your other bathroom accessories.

Always check that your taps are compatible with your bath or basin.

An elegantly-shaped bidet which is both comfortable to use and attractively discreet.

Decoration and Colour

Bathroom decoration spans the entire gamut, from the sleek, white-tiled cube to the fantastic and frivolous. The style you choose is an opportunity to express your personality. Of course, there may be compromises to make if you have decided to refurbish rather than completely revamp your bathroom; your colour scheme, for example, will probably have to be built around that of the existing suite.

You may have a very clear idea in mind of how your bathroom should look. Will it be highly decorated with floral tile and fabric patterns, in the Victorian manner? Based around a black and white chequered pattern, popular in 1930s Art Deco rooms? Or perhaps a watery grotto in dark greens and blues?

The secret of a successful decorative scheme is attention to detail. For example, the smartness of a high-tech bathroom will be utterly destroyed by hanging floral curtains at the window. Venetian or roller blinds will look much more effective. Take care to ensure all your fittings are in matching colours - brass taps and a chrome mirror frame will do both a disservice.

Before you start any decoration work, check that all your surfaces are sound. Flaking paint should be rubbed down with sandpaper, cracks and holes should be filled, and loose tiles refixed. Old grouting can be dug out and replaced. For tiles in wet areas, buy a water-resistant grout - it is more expensive but the investment is well worthwhile.

Wall Coverings

Ceramic tiles are easily the most popular wall covering found in the bathroom. They are available in countless shapes, colours and patterns, are easy to apply and offer a durable, water- and stain-resistant, bright, easy-to-clean, finish. In the right setting, even the humble, square white tile can look stunning.

Their main drawback is that the grout tends to pick up stains. Scrubbing in between tiles with an old toothbrush will remove most discoloration, and there are now products on the market devised specifically for lifting off dirt. However, if stains persist, it is advisable to scrape out old grout and replace it with new.

Tiles can be used in a multitude of different ways to create the look you want. You may choose one plain colour or an elaborately patterned effect. An unusual and interesting pattern can be created by mixing up an assortment of plain or plain and patterned tiles. For a really eye-catching effect, fix square tiles on their ends to form a diamond shape. Mosaics, many of which are sold in ready-assembled panels, are unusual and stylish used on both walls and floors.

If you choose to tile your bath panel or walls and units that enclose pipe work or the lavatory cistern, ensure you can gain access for maintenance. This is achieved either by tiling an entire panel and then grouting in into place, or by tiling a panel and fixing it with round-head mirror screws. Always buy a few spare tiles in case of damage during installation or for future repairs.

The unusual, pivoted circular window makes a wonderful focal point to this jolly room. The rich blue- and gold-starred walls provide a colour theme continued in the decorative corner unit and the ceiling. The ideal setting for an exotic, candle-lit bath time.

Wood panelling kits are now stocked by many hardware stores. You can opt for square panels or a tongue-and-groove style. This sort of finish works well when fixed from floor to ceiling, or from floor to counter height to give you a half-panelled room. The wood is usually sold unfinished so you can choose whether to varnish or paint it.

If you are feeling adventurous, you may consider searching out old, reclaimed wood panelling from an architectural salvage yard. Much of this material has been stripped from decommissioned churches and can look extremely handsome in a bathroom.

Wallpaper is a popular choice in bathrooms as it can soften the hardness of sanitary ware and ceramic tiles. Due to the inevitability of condensation and water splashes in the bathroom, it is always wise to choose a vinyl paper which is coated with a water-resistant seal.

Paint is often all that is needed to transform a bathroom. Walls must be sound and free from damp, flaking paint and peeling wallpaper. While paint, especially oil-based, is durable, it is not recommended for wall areas most exposed to water - such as those directly above the bath, by the shower or behind the basin.

When it comes to applying the paint, if you want to be adventurous, you could try a mural or any one of the many paint effects that have become so popular in recent years. Dozens of books have been published with step-by-step instructions on such techniques as rag rolling, sponging and dragging. Stippling is a particularly delicate and intriguing finish.

Of course, among the most popular of paint decoration effects is stencilling. There are numerous specialist companies producing a vast array of stencil designs - from simple flowers, sea creatures and shells to complex and intricate effects - which are available, complete with full instructions, from good hardware and department stores. Once again, always check the manufacturer's instructions to ensure the paint you choose is suitable for use in the bathroom.

Colour Schemes

Once you have chosen a decorative theme, you can start to make decisions about the colours. You will certainly have thought long and hard about schemes and may have made some colour decisions already by choosing the sanitary ware. Selecting the colours for walls, ceiling and woodwork is great fun. If ever you are unsure about a colour, buy a couple of test pots and experiment.

Personal preference and association are powerful ingredients in making your choice. If you have fond memories of a childhood bathroom, for example, you may well want to create a similar colour scheme. If you do not have a particular colour in mind, it is a good idea to build a scheme around some stunning tiles you have discovered, reclaimed wood panelling, a favourite painting or perhaps a suitable theme such as the seaside (see 'Theme Bathrooms', page 40).

In practical terms, you should take into account the colours of the items already chosen: blues, yellows and white, for example, look wonderful with natural wood finishes; blue and white are clean and crisp; black and white looks extremely smart with a white bathroom suite; dark blue is rich and handsome; black is sexy, and so on.

Take careful note of the natural light in your room. North-facing bathrooms will receive no direct sunlight; east-facing rooms receive the weak morning sun; west-facing bathrooms will get the rich evening light, while those that are south-facing will receive direct sunlight through most of the day. To make a room feel warmer, choose from the red end of the spectrum, or choose soft neutrals such as cream and ivory. For a cooler effect, use blues and greens.

It is possible to improve the quality of light by replacing old, obscured glass with clear or slightly tinted panes. This, however, is only recommended if your bathroom is not overlooked. Should you have eagle-eyed neighbours, consider replacing the thick, old glass with a modern etched pane. Etching gives a soft, pale, frosted effect; a good glazier will be able to etch the glass for you. A stained-glass window will also deter any onlookers and can provide an intriguing focus for the room.

An ill-lit room may look at its best simply in white - white does, in fact, suit almost every bathroom because of its associations with cleanliness, hygiene and purity.

The complete antithesis of the surgically pristine white-tiled shower, this colourful cubicle will set the pulse racing and has plenty of room for a vigorous scrub to start the day.

Lighting

Water and electricity are a very dangerous combination and, therefore, any work carried out on bathroom lighting should be completed by a professional. It is also important to formulate your ideas about lighting schemes and plan ahead before you start work on a task such as wall tiling - wires may have to be traced into the wall. Good lighting is always a wise investment. It can enhance the room's decor and help create its atmosphere. The wrong type of lighting will drastically reduce your enjoyment of the room. It would be a terrible shame to spoil all your hard work by installing inappropriate lights.

Tungsten This is the light provided by regular domestic bulbs. The clear bulb will cast a warm, slightly yellow light. In addition, there are many pearl-finished and coloured bulbs to help you to create the right mood. It is also available in strips. These make excellent bathroom lighting as the unit is sealed and protected from condensation and steam.

Fluorescent is most commonly available as strip or tube lighting. Fluorescent tubes are available in a wide variety of lengths; they are long lasting and energy efficient and therefore cheap to run. Fluorescent light is characterised by its blue-white colour which is rather harsh on the eye. Ideally, this type of lighting should be fixed behind a shield - a cupboard pelmet, for example.

Halogen is low-voltage and emits a wonderful, crisp, white, sparkling light. This type of lighting has become increasingly popular in recent years and is now available in a variety of styles: recessed lights, single-fitting lamps and small tracks sprouting a number of bulbs. The bulbs are sold as spots, which cast a small pool of concentrated light, or wide angle, which shed larger pools with softer edges.

The drawbacks are that the bulbs, while long lasting if treated with care, are fragile and expensive. Look out for those with a protective glass shield to protect against condensation and steam. Do bear in mind that the installation of halogen lights is a specialist task as they require transformers. Usually in the form of small, heavy boxes or cigar-shaped tubes, these transform the powerful mains into a low-voltage supply. They can be fitted either close to the light source or remotely. They usually emit a slight hum, and so are best placed inside the ceiling recess or, perhaps, a cupboard.

Lighting Design

As a general rule you will need two types of lighting. Firstly, a room wash, and secondly, task lights over the wash-hand basin and mirror. Separate switches are advisable. When deciding on a lighting scheme for a bathroom, your design should take into account the fact that bulbs should not be exposed to damaging steam and condensation.

On the subject of overall room lighting, the overhead pendant fitting rarely adds anything to a bathroom unless it is adequately supplemented by wall lights and task lights. It can shed a rather stark light and will cause shadows. Fluorescent is not the ideal choice either; it is harsh and can be horribly unflattering.

For a softer, all-round glow, consider wall lights. These are available in many styles, from copies of Victorian gas lamps to contemporary, moulded ceramic up lighters. Choose fittings to suit the rest of your decor and fix them above eye-level to give a gentle, inviting glow. This sort of lighting works extremely well with pale colour schemes and natural materials such as wood and cork. Remember that dark colours absorb light and will probably need more light fittings than reflective white or pale colour schemes.

For dramatic and sparkly lighting, take a look at the choice of ceiling-recessed fittings available. Recessed tungsten and low-voltage halogen lights complement fresh and bright colours and lots of ceramic tiling. They are offered with a fixed-position beam or a moveable 'eyeball' centre that can be directed to wash a wall with light or to highlight specific objects or areas.

Recessed lights are a particularly good idea in bathrooms with low ceilings and can be bought in sealed units that protect lamps from water splashes and condensation. If you have a high ceiling, an excellent way of throwing light upwards is to fix small up lighters above wall-fixed units or on high shelves. Light will bounce off the ceiling and fall as a soft glow.

For basin and mirror task lighting, small strips of tungsten work well. Just like

kitchen lighting, these can be fixed behind baffles to prevent glare. Low-voltage halogen is also excellent and, because of its pure, crisp light, will make chrome, glass and ceramic really sparkle. For the ultimate in glitz and glamour, you could opt for a theatrical dressing room-style mirror framed by a halo of light bulbs.

All bathroom lights are most safely operated by a pull-cord. If you choose to fit a dimmer switch, you will probably be advised by your electrician to fit it outside and away from all possible contact with water. Lastly, do not forget candles. Obviously, these are not

recommended for everyday lighting; however, the diffused quality of candlelight is difficult to beat, especially for a really relaxing, soothing soak.

For plenty of glamour, this double basin and large mirror with inset bulbs should appeal to anyone with a passion for theatrical settings. The crimson towels and accessories stand in dramatic contrast with the cream coloured walls and storage unit.

Flooring

Bathrooms, especially family ones, are subjected to tremendous wear and tear and the flooring you choose must be tough and, above all, waterproof or fitted with efficient drainage. Even where money is no object, some finishes, such as stone, may be out of the question because your floor simply cannot take the weight. Very heavy materials should only be laid on a solid concrete floor or there is a danger of causing structural damage. Ceramic and terracotta tiles are also best laid on a solid floor, partly because of their weight but also because, if laid on a wood base, the joints will move and crack. It is sensible to check with a builder or supplier if you are considering one of these types of flooring.

Your choice of colour and pattern is also important. A plain-coloured floor, especially if it is white, will show every mark. A flecked design or small pattern will spare you hours of cleaning. That said, floors with a light-coloured base will brighten a room, while darker shades will close it in.

Lively patterns can overwhelm a bathroom. If you are lucky enough to have a large room, it could look stunning with a bold black and white chequerboard design; whereas this treatment could completely overpower a small bathroom. In smaller spaces, a plain finish is generally preferable: so, if in doubt, keep it simple. A number of types of flooring are suitable for the bathroom.

Wood

If you are lucky enough to have good floorboards (most are hardwearing pine), you have the opportunity to achieve a marvellous stripped and varnished finish at a reasonable cost. You could try a subtle pattern by choosing from some of the many colours of wood stain that are now available.

The advantages of timber are that it is durable, smart, warm and can improve with age. The disadvantages are that it can dent and scar if damaged by heavy or sharp objects, and, unless thoroughly sealed with a durable varnish (yacht varnish is the best in these circumstances as it has been developed to be water tight), it may not wear well if regularly

doused with water. It is a good idea to use a rug in front of the bath or shower to soak up most of the water. Also, wood is not particularly good at providing sound proofing (although filling spaces between joists with an acoustic dampener or simple loft insulation is fairly inexpensive and can successfully prevent noise from travelling), and it requires some maintenance such as occasional revarnishing.

You will probably need to replace some of the damaged boards and hire a professional sanding machine to lift off the worn and grubby top surface. If new boards are a lighter colour than your existing ones, you can 'age' them by painting on a couple of coats of cold, black tea or by using a wood stain. Once you have achieved an even surface and cleared away all the dust, paint the boards with several coats of tough varnish for a rich, glowing, and hardwearing finish. For a limed effect, paint the sanded boards with watered-down white

Demonstrating that the bath doesn't have to be hidden behind a plain panel, this ornately embellished roll top tub is a celebration of Victorian detailing. It sits on a neat blue and white chequered floor and is fed by free-standing chrome taps and shower.

emulsion and then protect with matte varnish. When painting or varnishing floors, make sure you start at the corner furthest from the door so that you do not have to walk across the wet surface to leave the room.

If all this sounds like too much effort, a good-quality wood finish is possible with the timber veneer and laminate packs available in every hardware store. The laminate finish is virtually indestructible: it resists damage from grit and sharp heels, stains and cigarette burns. These packs are sold in a variety of styles and colours - from prepared wood 'tiles' (composed of small timber strips fixed on to a backing material) to lengths of tongue-and-groove. The tiles will give the effect of a parquet or wood-block floor, while the tongue-and-groove system will give the impression of neat boards. These packs are sold either ready varnished or untreated so that you may stain and varnish them as you choose. The secret of achieving a professional finish is to ensure that your existing floor is completely flat and firm. Most of the "do-it-yourself" packs are best fixed on a layer of sturdy chipboard or hardboard; advice will be given in the accompanying instructions. When working on any sort of wood flooring for the bathroom, always ensure the

joints are completely sealed - water seeping can cause serious structural damage.

Vinyl

This incredibly tough material is stain resistant, waterproof, easy to wash clean and warm to the touch. It is available in a wide range of thicknesses and prices. As a general rule, the thicker it is the more it costs. Vinyl flooring is available either in sheet or tile form, cushioned or solid. It is manufactured in a vast array of finishes including a convincing wood-block effect, wood strips, marble, limestone, granite, brick and slate. Many decorative borders and special patterned inserts are available. The major manufacturers offer a design and installation service which means that you can have your floor tailor-made.

To achieve the best results with this material, it is essential to start with a well-prepared, flat base - chipboard or hardboard are ideal. Using a recommended adhesive, both tiles and sheets are easy to lay and are virtually maintenance-free.

Linoleum

This finish shares many of the properties of vinyl. It is warm, stain resistant, durable, easily washable, and is also available in sheet or tile form. In recent

years linoleum has enjoyed a revival because it is manufactured with natural materials such as cork, linseed oil, wood and resins. As demand has increased, so has the choice of colours and patterns.

Cork Tiles

Easy to clean, warm under foot, inexpensive, tough, easy to lay and with an intriguing, mottled finish, cork has remained popular for years. It has the added advantage of being a natural substance that is grown as a renewable material.

As with wood and vinyl, the answer to a perfect finish lies in meticulous preparation. Cork tiles do not sit happily on uneven floors: they must be dry and flat. Spread the recommended adhesive over the entire surface of the tile to ensure a good, firm bond. Loose corners are easily damaged and will soon look ugly.

Tiles are sold ready prepared with a PVC coating, or in their natural state. The natural tiles are slightly easier to cut and fit to awkward shapes and may then be coloured. Really thorough sealing is essential to ensure resistance to water penetration and for long life. Place a rug in front of the bath or shower to soak up most of the water.

Ceramic Tiles

The choice of ceramic tiles is enormous and includes hundreds of beautiful colours and patterns. These tiles are hardwearing, easily cleaned and are available in price ranges to suit almost all budgets. Their disadvantages are that they are hard, cold under foot and noisy. They also become slippery when wet, which is not good news in the bathroom; however, some slip-resistant finishes are available - check with your supplier.

Almost without exception, ceramic tiles should be laid on solid floors, as they are likely to be too heavy to be laid on top of timber joists. For the very best results, especially in large areas, these tiles should be laid professionally.

Hard Finishes

Stone, slate and marble can look gorgeous. Stone flags acquire a glorious patina with age, slate has a sleek, understated grandeur, and marble can look incredibly luxurious. All are extremely hardwearing and expensive. They are also hard, cold and tend to be noisy.

The good news for those with timber floors is that light-weight marble and slate slips or tiles are increasingly available and offer a less-expensive option to the heavier slabs.

Terrazzo

An aggregate composed of stone and glass chippings and concrete, terrazzo is tough, colourful and available in tiles or slabs. This type of flooring is best laid on solid floors because of its heavy weight; and, once again, it is worth paying an expert to fit this kind of flooring.

Carpet Some people have an intense dislike of cold floors and far prefer to carpet their bathroom. Carpet is warm and soft under foot and available in extensive ranges. If you decide on this type of flooring, you should always buy a quality recommended for use in the bathroom. It is also a good idea to place a rug in front of the bath and shower to soak up excess water.

Rubber stud flooring is practical and unusual. The finish prevents slipping - always a problem in a smooth-finish floor - and is waterproof. A nautical theme is picked up in the fish pattern on the tiles and in the model boat.

Theme Bathrooms

Bathroom design based around a specific idea or theme can be particularly successful, giving the whole room an integrity. Indeed, the bathroom is an appropriate part of the house in which to indulge a design whim or fantasy, and where a sense of fun is also in keeping.

On the Crest of a Wave

Seaside and nautical themes work extremely well in the bathroom and allow plenty of opportunity for amusing touches.

The first step is to decide on your marine theme: will it be based on boat interiors, the seaside, underwater caves, or perhaps the flora and fauna of the coast?

Rub-a-dub-dub

Classic white is difficult to beat for your bathroom sanitary ware, as it will lend itself to just about any nautical theme. If your heart is set on introducing colour here, then pale blue or green or a sandy shade are the most suitable. The most flamboyant tastes can be satisfied by choosing one of the suites available with shell-like, scalloped decoration.

An unusual idea for your bath is to give it boat-like panelling, easily achieved by fixing long, horizontal planks to the side.

These can be left in their natural state and given a stained and varnished finish, or can be painted seaside colours - pale blue, aqua or white.

Give the lavatory a wooden seat and cover, too.

Pushing the Boat Out

Tongue-and-groove panelled walls can lend a distinctly seaside atmosphere. This finish can evoke the feeling of being in the cabin of a ship or, perhaps, taking it easy in a beach hut. Once again, the wood will look handsome if given a simple coat of varnish or a coat of pale paint. If you really want to go overboard, fit tongue-and-groove on the ceiling too.

If your room is half-panelled to dado height, you may like to add a decorative wallpaper border - there is plenty of choice available with designs incorporating shells, sea horses, fishes, pebbles, boats and waves. A similar array of effects is available as stencils which, of

course, you could paint on to walls, the bath panel, cupboards, fabric blinds and even the floor.

Many manufacturers produce water-resistant vinyl wallpapers with seaside-related patterns but, for a really unusual wall covering, collect piles of new or old maps and paste them to the walls. To prevent damage by steam and condensation, give them a coat of clear or yellowish varnish.

There is a wonderful choice of ceramic tiles with all sorts of seaside, marine and nautical patterns; one manufacturer, for example, produces a collection of deep blue tiles sporting life-like pictures of whales, dolphins and porpoises. Finish your room with these and you will know what it is like to be a scuba diver. It is even possible to buy radiators in the shape of dolphins! If you have existing plain tiles, you might like to brighten them up and paint them with a seaside mural or patterns (see pages 46-7).

Shells are of great decorative value. By selecting just a few spectacular specimens, they can be used in an understated way to add lashings of style. Pretty, creamy shells have been stuck to the picture frame and the shell theme is continued on the lampshade.

This powerful red, white and blue nautical theme makes bath time great fun. Accessories including the rope, brass clock, porthole mirror and rubber fishes add the finishing touches. Red, white and blue towels are a must.

For paint finishes, aquamarine, white and sand are essential beach colours. Add a splash of brighter colour by painting walls with bold deck chair stripes in navy and white, crimson and navy, or emerald and sunshine yellow. You may even be lucky enough to find a vinyl wallpaper in one of these sunny colour combinations.

To complete the effect, why not paint your ceiling sky blue dotted with fluffy white clouds and, maybe, hang up a wooden seagull?

All Hands on Deck

Turn your floor into the deck of a ship with glossy varnished boards, or perhaps you would prefer a seaside look with sandy-coloured vinyl. Large vinyl manufacturers will be able to design you a pattern using yellow and blue that will resemble waves lapping the shore. Mosaics look chic in this type of setting, too.

Ship Shape

Now comes the part where you really can create a big splash. The range of bathroom accessories is enormous: from rubber ducks, shell-shaped soap, coils of rope and bubble-bath-filled boats, to loofahs, a ship in a bottle, deck-chair striped towels, a disused lobster pot or an elegant piece of driftwood. A large seaside painting, poster or print will act as a focus of attention.

Natural shells are among the most charming and versatile accessories. They can be stuck to all manner of surfaces to create intriguing patterns: perhaps you could design shell panels for your bath, a decorative border round the top of the room, or around a mirror frame?

If you have opted for the boat theme, how about turning a simple pine box into a pirate's chest, ideal for storing bath-time toys, towels or dirty linen? All you will need is a stout brass

lock and a handful of brass corner pieces that are easily screwed into place. You could also line the interior with navy-and-white striped or red-and-white polka dot paper and paint a skull-and-crossbones on the top. Chrome or brass-framed porthole mirrors are fun too. You could fit a porthole-shaped window in the door or wall.

For authentic lighting, fit a couple of bulkhead lights. These are ideal in the bathroom as they are sealed and protected from water splashes, condensation and seam.

An ingenious coiled rope mat, a border of pretty shells, and pictures of fishermen and boats. Lying in the bath, which has been given a striking mottled paint effect to match the door, it's possible to float away into the clouds painted on the walls.

The beach-hut theme can be carried through with a couple of well-chosen items of furniture. A basket-weave chair and small table, perhaps. A wicker laundry basket and wooden, slatted blinds will also look splendid.

Project 1
• • • • • • • • •

Distressing bathroom furniture

This is an effect that works well on almost all wood-built furniture, from chairs and shelves to wardrobes and cupboards. The distressed finish is all about creating a well-worn, lived-in look that can be particularly effective in bathrooms with a seaside theme.

Tools and Materials

- water-based emulsion paint
- paintbrush
- sandpaper
- wire brush
- matt varnish (optional)

1 Ensure that the piece of furniture is sound and repair any damage you may find.

To repair joints that have worked loose, remove all rusty nails and clean out old glue. If old adhesive proves difficult to shift, place a hot, damp cloth over the area to soften. Sandpaper the surfaces of the joint. Re-nail and glue the joint; clamp it or place it under heavy weights overnight while the glue dries. Check that the feet are level. If not, they should either be built up or sawn to match. Ensure shelves are firmly fixed in place. They can be strengthened by fixing additional blocks or strips of wood underneath for support. If possible, remove all handles before painting.

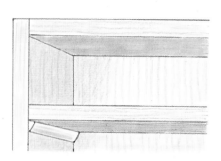

2 Paint the furniture with one coat of water-based emulsion and leave it to dry thoroughly.

If you like a limed look, choose a pale colour and thin down the mixture: around one part paint to three or four parts water is usually about right. The mixture depends on the thickness of the paint however; after thinning, the consistency should be thin and runny. Paint on just one coat of this mixture and leave to dry. To complete the effect, sandpaper the entire surface to reveal the grain. For a limed and distressed finish, also follow the next step.

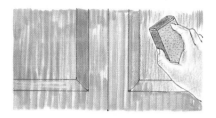

3 Using sandpaper and a wire brush, work away at the dry paint surface in the direction of the grain. Stop occasionally and stand back to see how close you are to achieving your desired effect. Remember that for authentic-looking distressing, most wear would show around handles and door knobs.

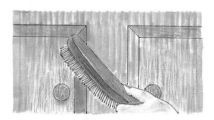

4 Replace the original handles, or choose others to match the rest of the room. If you want to protect the paint surface, add a coat of matt varnish. Alternatively, you can leave the furniture to collect its own genuine knocks and scratches.

Project 2
· · · · · · · · ·

Decorating plain tiles

This is a quick and simple way of brightening up old plain tiles. Paint on a pattern or, if you have children, let them make up their own designs. You will find everything you need at a good art and craft suppliers.

Tools and Materials

- masking tape
- old newspapers
- drawing paper
- a selection of brightly-coloured ceramic paints
- 2 or 3 watercolour paintbrushes
- clear ceramic varnish

1 Ensure the tiles are clean. Wash them down with a bathroom cleaner or liquid detergent and rinse well. Leave the tiles to dry thoroughly before you start work.

2 Using the masking tape and newspaper, mask off the wall directly around the tiles to protect it from misdirected paint spatters. Also cover the taps and basin.

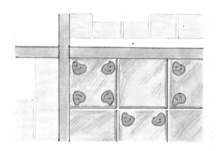

3 Work out the design on sheets of paper. They can, of course, be as simple or as complex as you like. You could try a small mural - waves, Noah's ark, sea creatures, a shipwreck - or a series of designs for individual tiles featuring boats, fishes, sea horses, shells, and so on. Once you have the outline of the shapes, and the pattern, choose the colours of each image. The proportion of the design to the area being painted is important. Create a design which does not overpower you.

Free-hand painting is not difficult — you just need confidence and a steady hand. Have a rag handy to wipe out any shapes which do not work the first time.

4 Carefully paint the designs on to the tiles. Work from left to right if you are right-handed, and from right to left if you are left-handed; this will ensure that you do not smudge the wet paint as you work. Leave to dry thoroughly.

5 To protect the paintings from water splashes, seal the surface with a coat of clear ceramic varnish.

Project 3
• • • • • • • •

Stencilling a pattern on a wooden floor

Wooden floors have tremendous charm and the timber finishes available are many and varied - from natural, waxed woods to varnished, stained and painted boards. A stencilled pattern is both attractive and unusual – and, with a little patience, is surprisingly easy to achieve.

Before you start, ensure the wood surface is smooth and grit, grease and dust free. Remove all nails. If the floor has recently been uncovered or is extremely worn, you may need to level the surface and clean it up with a professional sanding machine - these are available for hire from most hardware stores and hire shops.

Tools and Materials

- stencil – the patterns available are numerous, and even the most simple ones can look extremely effective
- stencil brush
- pencil
- ruler
- stencil paint recommended for wood
- sandpaper or hand-held sander
- clear varnish

1 Measure up your room and draw a floor plan, marking in the fixed items such as lavatory, bath and cupboards. It is a good idea to do this on graph paper. Decide on your stencil and, using a pencil, mark the position of your pattern on the floor plan. Once you are happy with the design, use your pencil to mark approximately where the stencils will appear on the floor.

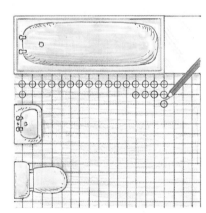

2 To paint, start at the far corner of the room and work back towards the door (it would be awful to ruin your hard work by stepping on wet paint). If you are unfamiliar with using stencils, it's a good idea to hold them in place with masking tape at the corners.

Apply the paint with a stencil brush. Remember to be sparing – too much will seep underneath the stencil and spoil the pattern.

3 After painting, carefully peel back the stencil to reveal the pattern. Start the process again until the design is complete.

4 When stencilling is finished, leave to dry thoroughly then lightly sand the entire floor surface with fine grain sand paper to remove any surface inequalities, dust and grit. Brush carefully and thoroughly and then add a coat of protective varnish. You will achieve a much more professional finish by applying two thin layers rather than one thick one.

Project 4
· · · · · · · · ·

Tiling behind the wash-hand basin

You do not need any experience in 'do-it-yourself' to tile a small area like this. If you follow the simple instructions below, with a little care and patience you will end up with a really professional-looking job.

Measure the space to be tiled to estimate how many tiles you will need to buy. It is always a good idea to buy a few spares just in case you break a couple while fixing them, or you may need replacements later on. When buying the adhesive and grout, read the instructions carefully to make sure you have the right type and quantity.

The key to success is good preparation. Before you start work, make sure you have all the tools and materials to hand. Also check that you have plenty of time so that you do not need to rush to complete the job.

2 Using a pencil and the wood battens, mark out the area to be tiled. Draw a grid on the wall of tile positions, leaving grouting space of around 3mm (1/8 in) between each tile. An important consideration here is that the top row is composed of whole tiles - cut tiles along the top will look messy. Use the spirit level to ensure the lines are level. Using small nails or pins, fix one of the battens along the lowest horizontal line. The tiling between this batten and the basin will be completed at the end of the job. A vertical batten also helps to keep the lines straight. Both battens will be removed when the job is complete.

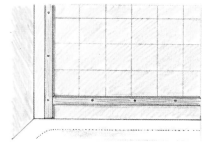

Tools and Materials

- pencil
- ruler
- two wooden battens, about 3cm x 12mm (1½ x ½in) and long enough to frame one side and the length of the area to be tiled
- spirit level
- small nails or pins
- tile adhesive (check that the pack includes a spreader)
- tiles (as estimated, plus a few spares)
- tile cutter
- pack of tile spacers
- water-resistant grout

1 Ensure the area of wall to be tiled is sound and smooth. Remove all traces of old tiles or wallpaper, chip off any loose paint or plaster, fill cracks and holes with a plaster filler and smooth with sandpaper.

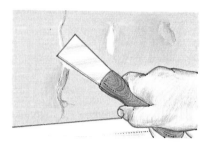

3 Most tile adhesive is sold with a spreader (a flat piece of plastic with one notched edge) inside the pack. Use this tool to spread adhesive directly on to the wall The adhesive should generally be around 3mm (1/8 in) deep, but check directions for recommended thickness. When you are tiling a large area, apply adhesive in sections of around 1 square metre (9 square feet) at a time.

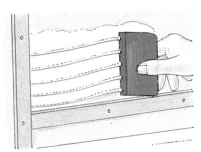

4 Lay the first tile at the right-angled corner made by the two battens. Press firmly into place. Continue along the horizontal line, using spacers between each tile. Check that the tiles in the first row are firmly stuck before starting on the line above.

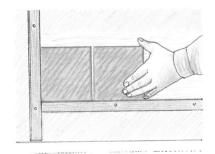

5 Allow the adhesive to dry for a day before filling tile gaps with grout. Ensure the grout is pressed firmly into the gaps and remove any excess with a damp cloth. Once the grout has dried, prise off the battens and fill any holes made by the pins. Finish the job by completing the last line of tiling and grouting.

Project 5
• • • • • • • •

Painting a wall frieze

A colourful frieze is easy to paint, inexpensive and can look dazzling. Try stencilling a pattern or, for added charm, hand drawing your own designs.

Tools and Materials

- pencil
- stencils
- masking tape
- 6mm (¼ in) and 12mm (½ in) watercolour brushes or stencil brushes
- emulsion or stencil paint suitable for bathrooms

1 For the best possible results, set aside plenty of time for thorough preparation. Ensure the wall surface is smooth and sound - take care to remove any flaking paint and glue any wallpaper joints that may have come unstuck. Use filler to repair any holes and sand to a smooth finish.

2 For both a hand drawn and a stencilled border, mark out with a pencil the area to be decorated. If you plan to give the frieze a coloured background, this is the time to do that. Let the paint dry before moving on to the next stage.

3 In the case of a hand drawn design, it is a good idea to pencil in the entire outline to act as a painting guide. This will also give you the opportunity to see the design and make adjustments before you start applying paint. Avoid the temptation to try very complex designs - simple can also be effective. A light pencil outline will be sufficient - heavy lines may prove difficult to cover or remove. For stencils, lightly pencil mark where the stencil pattern will appear.

4 Once you are happy with your design, you can start painting. For hand-drawn designs, work from left to right if you are right handed to avoid smudging your work. Allow plenty of time for paint to dry before laying another colour on top. When stencilling, hold the stencil in place with masking tape as you paint. Paint should be applied sparingly to avoid smudging. Remove the stencil carefully from the wall and wipe away any excess paint from the back before sticking it on the wall again. Once the paint has dried you can protect the frieze from water splashes with a coat of clear varnish.

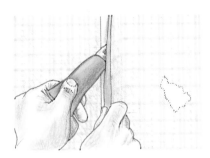

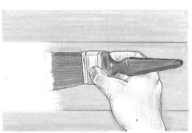

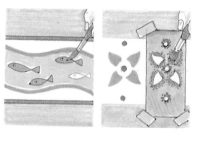

Project 6
· · · · · · · · ·

Making a shelf

This is an incredibly useful way to store a couple of towels within easy reach of the bath or shower. The small, integral shelf provides additional storage space for toiletries.

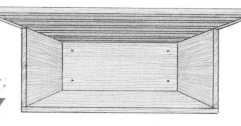

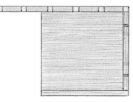

Tools and Materials

- one 168cm (5ft 8in) length of 24cm x 12mm (9½ x ½in) plywood
- one 440cm (14ft 8in) length of 12 x 12mm (½ x ½in) pine
- saw
- electric or hand drill
- nails
- hammer
- wood glue
- sandpaper
- paint or varnish
- rawl plugs
- screws

1 Saw the the 240cm x 12mm (9½ x ½in) plywood length into four pieces: two each of 60cm (24 in) for the shelf bottom and back; and two each 22.5cm (9 in), for the sides. Drill four holes in the back section 5cm (2 in) in from the corners to fix the shelf to the wall. Cut the 12 x 12mm (½ x ½in) pine into two 40cm (16 in) lengths for the sides, and six 57.5cm (23 in) lengths for the slats.

2 Begin to assemble the unit by fixing the two 60cm (24 in) lengths of shelving along their longest sides to make an L-shape, using nails and glue. The shortest part of the 'L' is the back panel with its four holes. Nail and glue the side pieces in place. You now have a two-sided box.

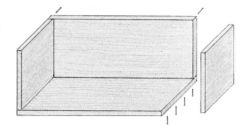

3 To make the top section, lay the slats between the two side rails, spacing them at regular intervals of approximately 8.5cm (3¾in). Nail and glue and leave to set firmly.

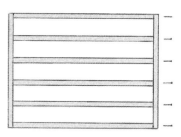

4 Complete by using nails and glue to fix the two sections together. Once the glue has dried, sandpaper all the surfaces and finish with paint or varnish.

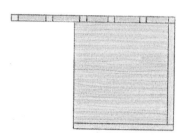

5 Select the most convenient area for the shelf and check that the wall is sound as it will need the strength to carry the weight of the rack and its contents. Walls constructed of brick and plaster are ideal. Thin wood or plasterboard partitions will not be able to support the weight.

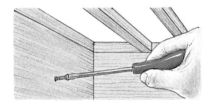

6 To fix the shelf to the wall, hold it in place and mark where the holes are on the wall with a pencil.

Make sure the drill bit is the correct size for the rawl plugs you are using. Drill holes and push in the plugs. Hold up the shelf again and drive screws into the rawl plugs.

Project 7
•••••••••

Panelling in the bathroom

A classic in bathroom design, tongue-and-groove panelling looks fabulous and it is also an excellent way to hide ugly pipes and disguise old tiles or uneven walls. Rooms are usually panelled either from floor to dado height, or from floor to ceiling.

Tongue-and-groove is surprisingly easy to fit and it comes in a variety of materials and finishes; among the most versatile is pine - it can be painted or varnished in any colour you choose. Measure your bathroom carefully.

Tools and Materials

- 5 x 5cm (2 x 2 in) softwood battens (buy larger battens if you are panelling over pipe work that protrudes more than 5cm (2 in).
- plumb line or spirit level
- screws or nails
- hammer
- sufficient tongue-and-groove panelling
- lost-head nails
- paint or varnish

1 Remove the skirting board and the picture rail – these can be replaced later, if desired.

2 Fix the battens to the wall. If the wall is uneven, you will need to use extra pieces of thin wood or hardboard behind the batten to keep it level and straight. Use a spirit level when fixing battens - good attention to detail at this stage will ensure the best possible finish. If you are fitting the boards vertically, then battens are fixed horizontally. It is best to leave a small gap - around 2.5-5cm (1-2in) from the floor and ceiling - when fitting top and bottom battens. If you nail boards too close to the end, the wood may split. Fix the battens at intervals of around 50-60cm (20-24in).

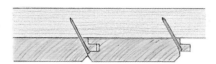

3 Starting at the left side of the wall (alternatively, if you have boards which are sold with metal fixing clips, see Step 4), place the first board with its groove facing left. Use a plumb line or spirit level to ensure it is completely vertical. Through the face of the board, screw or nail into position, sinking the head of the fixing so that the hole can be filled and disguised. Once the first board is straight and secure, slot in the next. All subsequent boards can be fixed in place with invisible nailing - lost-head nails are hammered into the tongue at an angle, as shown. As their name implies, these nails can be knocked completely into the timber allowing the next board to fit neatly over the tongue.

4 Some packs of tongue-and-groove boards are sold with metal fixing clips. To use these, you must fix the boards with the tongue facing to the left. The first, corner board must have the tongue sawn or planed off so that it will fit firmly against the wall. The clips then slot into the groove and hold the next board in place.

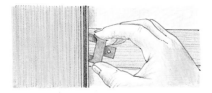

5 If the panelling covers pipes, it is usually a good idea to make it possible to remove a couple of boards for maintenance. To achieve this, saw or plane off the tongues (this makes them easy to lift out) from a couple of boards and fix them in place using screws. Sink the screw heads a couple of millimetres beneath the surface of boards and plug the holes with filler.

6 Complete the job by replacing skirting, if desired, and finish with the chosen paint or varnish.

Project 8
· · · · · · · ·

Glass effects

This is a simply brilliant way of giving plain glass in a window or a door a frosted look, which will ensure privacy in the bathroom without excluding natural light. It is even possible to add a simple stencilled pattern after the frosting is complete. The design could pick up decorative details from elsewhere in the bathroom, or be a new element in its own right.

Tools and Materials

- soapy water
- methylated spirit
- matt or eggshell varnish
- gloss or eggshell paint
- paintbrush
- stencil and stencil brush

1 Prepare the plain glass surface by scraping off any paint or varnish splashes that may have ended up on the pane. Then, with soapy water, thoroughly wash down the area to be painted. When dry, wipe over with methylated spirit on a soft, lint-free cotton cloth so that the area is free of all dust and fibres.

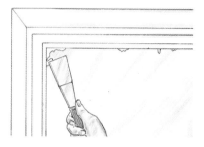

2 To make the 'frosting' mix ten parts of clear matt or eggshell varnish with one part of the chosen gloss or eggshell paint colour. It is obviously best to use a pale tint of colour so that light is not obscured from the bathroom. Paint this on to the glass in a light, even coat. Allow to dry completely.

3 To apply the stencil pattern, use undiluted gloss or eggshell paint and apply sparingly to avoid runs and splashes.

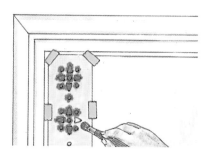

4 Carefully peel off the stencil and allow the paint to dry. If the stencil is to be used repeatedly, make sure to wipe the back clean of paint smears before re-applying it with masking tape.

Project 9
· · · · · · · ·

Stencilling a cupboard

Stencilling has remained an incredibly popular and simple way of decorating plain furniture, walls and floors. A stencilled pattern on a bathroom cupboard can pick up on tile designs, wallpaper patterns, a seaside theme or an image from a favourite painting.

There are, of course, dozens of excellent, ready-made stencil patterns; do not forget, however, that you can easily design and cut own patterns. To make stencils, buy a sheet of stencil paper (available from art and craft suppliers), draw the design on it and, using a sharp scalpel, cut it out.

Tools and Materials

- pencil
- your chosen stencil
- masking tape
- emulsion paint in the chosen colour(s)
- old bowl or plate
- stencil brush (these have short, stiff bristles and are available from art and craft suppliers)

1 Ensure the surface to be stencilled is clean, dry and free from grease, dust or dirt. Once you have chosen the stencil pattern, decide exactly where it will appear; hold it up in several positions to make sure you have got it absolutely right. You could also trace the outline lightly in pencil, remove the stencil and step back to check that you are happy with the position.

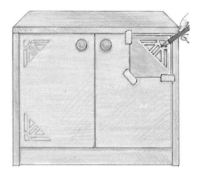

2 Fix the stencil in place using short strips of masking tape across the corners. Transfer a small quantity of emulsion paint from the tin to an old shallow bowl or plate. Dip just the end of the brush into the paint; take care not to overload the bristles as this can cause the paint to 'bleed' behind the stencil. Dab gently at the stencil area (as if you were stippling) and build up the colour to the required intensity.

If you intend to add a second colour, make sure the first coat is completely dry. Of course, you may want the colours to merge slightly - if so, add the second colour while the first is still slightly wet.

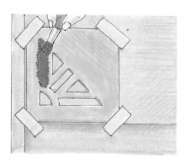

3 When the stippling is complete, remove the masking tape very gently and peel back the stencil from the wall, taking great care not to smudge the image. Using a soft paper towel or cloth, wipe any traces of paint from the back of the stencil before using it again. Continue until the design is finished.

Project 10
• • • • • • • • • •

Making a wooden slat mat

A wooden slat mat makes an unusual and practical feature in the bathroom. You won't have to stand around on cold floors when you get out of the shower or bath. And the natural wood looks great as part of a seaside or boat theme.

Tools and Materials

- 100 mm (4 ins) x 12 mm (½inch) pine boards - lengths required are 2 x 260 mm (20½ins) long and 4 x 750 mm (30ins)
- wood glue
- 20 mm screws
- clear varnish

1 Carefully sand the boards to ensure they are smooth and splinter free. Take the four 750mm length pieces and lay them side by side leaving a space between each of approximately 35mm (1½ins). On top of these and at right angles, lay the two 260 mm lengths of timber approximately 350 mm (14 ins) apart. Mark their positions in pencil.

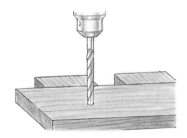

2 The screws are to be driven into the 260 mm timbers. When the slat mat is complete, these form the base. Mark their positions in pencil. To ensure the screws go into the wood easily and do not protrude and damage the bathroom floor, it is a good idea to start the hole to the depth of a couple of millimetres with a drill.

3 Before you fix the screws, lay all the lengths of wood in place and glue. Once the glue has dried, secure the slats with the screws, one to each slat.

4 To complete the slat mat, check that all screw heads are sunk below the wood surface and sand the entire unit. You can opt to paint the finished article - making sure you give it a coat of wood primer before adding the gloss or eggshell paint, or, as shown in our pictures, add matte or gloss varnish to seal the wood and show off the natural grain.

Index